1001 Leadership Tips for Emerging Leaders

Series One

101 Leadership Tips

by
Adeola Akintoye

www.adeolaakintoye.com

Dedication

To my Father, YHVH.

To equip and empower you to excel and thrive in your leadership journey.

Introduction

Everyone is a leader in one way or another, whether you are in a leadership position in an organisation, an expert in a technical profession, the first child of your parent, the head of a family or maybe people follow you because of your personality. You might be a leader because of your position or ability, but it does not necessarily mean you have a positive impact on people and in their lives.

Leaders who make a positive impact in their generation are those who inspire people directly or indirectly by the substance of their character and the quality of their work. Their impact goes beyond their own generation. They leave legacies for future generations as a result of the impact they make in peoples' lives. Inspirational leaders have more than technical competencies. They have the character, attitude and behaviour that underpin their technical skills, making them an inspiration to people. Their 'light' shines to those near and far. Their life and work add value to people. They become the salt of the earth and light of the world.

The "Leadership Tips Series" offers a wealth of practical wisdom and insights designed to empower emerging leaders and those seeking to make a positive impact in their organizations and communities.

The series equips leaders across

sectors with practical, actionable insights to strengthen their character, attitude, and decision-making skills. By blending real-world wisdom and theoretical knowledge, the series empowers leaders to inspire change, transform relationships, and foster growth within their teams and organizations. It's designed for daily reflection and application, making it a valuable tool for continuous personal and professional development across diverse leadership contexts.

Series One focus on key competency for a leader. Each leadership tip is followed by questions or statements for you to reflect on and respond to honestly.

The success of your leadership is dependent on you, your ability for critical self-assessment and the decision to make changes where and when necessary. Being an inspirational leader is not perfected in the classroom but experienced in our day-to-day relationships and attitude to our work.

Table of Contents

Authenticity

1. Be authentic. Be you, be positively different, do something different that sets you apart as a leader.

What gifts, talents, skills and abilities do I have that make me different?

Character

2. Be consistent. Your integrity depends on this.

Do I have the habit of changing my word and mind all the time?

3. Honesty is the key to credibility. If you get caught in a lie, your integrity and others' respect for you are gone.

Is it easy for me to lie?

4. Perseverance will see you through challenging times and build your character.

Do I give up easily when faced with a challenge?

5. Be disciplined in your attitude to work.

Am I disciplined when it comes to my work?

6. Let who you are on the outside reflect who you are inside. Don't be two-faced.

When I'm with people, do I speak the truth, or do I say what makes people happy?

7. Think positively. Get rid of negative thoughts and replace them with positive ones.

I will be positive even when I do not feel it.

8. Walk the talk. Practice what you preach. Let your 'yes' be yes and your 'no' be no. This is the essence of integrity.

Do I mean yes when I say yes and no when I say no?

9. Lead by your character. You can fool others in the short term, but your character will bear you out.

How is my character positively influencing other people?

10. Always be humble. Humility is the essence of a leader.

In what ways am I humble?

11. You need character, built by integrity, values and principles. Character makes a leader. Develop yours.

What would my family say about my character?

12.   Integrity is the core of a great leader.

Do I keep my word?

13. Control your temper.

What triggers my temper? I will stop and think before I react.

14. A leader must always be faithful in all things.

How can I demonstrate faithfulness?

15. Be determined to reach your goal.

How often do I procrastinate?

16. Lead with diligence.

How seriously do I take my responsibilities as a leader?

17. A leader's conduct must be honorable at all times.

Have I mis-used my position recently?

18. When leaders do the right thing, they silence the ignorance of foolish people.

What does doing the right thing mean to me?

Integrity

is the

core of a

great leader

Self reflection.

What will I;

Stop doing

_____

_____

Start doing

_____

_____

Communication

19. Use words as a tool. Listen to the words people use; it tells you what matters a lot to them.

What words does the person closest to me use most of the time? Why is that word important to him or her?

20. Listen to understand than to respond- S. Covey.

How do I avoid misunderstanding what people say?

21. Respond with the intention to gain understanding, rather than to make people feel stupid.

Do I under-value other people's contribution in a discussion?

22. Use few words to get your message across; many words confuse the message.

Do I go round in circles rather than going straight to the point?

Conflict Management

23. As much as possible, go for a win-win in negotiation and conflict resolution.

How good are my negotiation skills? Do I need training?

24. Never compromise your principles.

What are my principles?

25. Ask questions more often than give answers. It gets all the parties talking to one another.

What questions could I ask when dealing with a conflict situation?

26. Do not tell your peers off in front of their team.

How do I correct inaccuracies with facts, not opinion?

27. Couple power or influence with humility when there is a problem.

How would I attempt to influence people when there is a problem?

Decision making

28. Timing is critical; know when the time is perfect.

When would I know the time is perfect to act?

29.   Do not consider only an isolated event when making a decision. Always look at trends.

How do I reach conclusion on an issue?

30. Do not base your decision on one incident only. Consider all incidents.

Which one incident would make me take an instant decision?

31. Put yourself in other people's shoes before you make a decision that affects them.

Do I consider other people when I make decisions affecting them?

32. To make an effective decision, you need facts, information and good judgement.

Do I take time to get all the facts before making a decision? What would I do if I need to make an immediate decision?

33. Know the pros (positives) and cons (negatives) of every decision you make.

If the negatives of a decision are more than the positives, what would I do?

34. Great leaders take personal responsibility for the outcome of their decision and are accountable to their followers for delivering results.

What does accountability mean to me?

35. Stop waiting for the perfect condition.

When was the last time I took a risk for something or someone I believed in?

Determination

36.   To get to the peak of a mountain, you need to take one step at a time. One step will not get you to the top of a mountain, but many small steps will.

As you work towards your vision, just keep on taking those small steps.

37. Be focused on vision, goals and priorities.

I must keep my vision in my heart all the time.

Hard Work

38.   Do not be afraid of hard work; go the extra mile, be a self-starter and be self-motivated.

What keeps me motivated?

39. Do more than is expected.

Do I expect rewards for things I do for other people?

40. Work hard for your own and others' needs.

Am I willing to go the extra mile to achieve the results I desire?

Influencing

41. You influence by the substance of your character, adding value to people's lives and the quality of your work.
Character - develop it.
Value - define it.
Quality - build it.

What values would I not compromise?

42. Learn the art of influence.

Who was the last person I influenced to see or do things my way?

Self reflection.

What will I;

Stop doing

_____

_____

Start doing

_____

_____

Leadership

43. The leader who exercises power with honor will work from the inside out, starting with himself - Blaine Lee, The Power Principle

How do I lead myself?

44. Everyone is a leader. Leadership is about influence. We influence each other in one capacity or another (as a parent, friend or boss).

I am a leader because....

45. Leadership is about elevating others.

What do I do to elevate others around me?

46. A leader gives away power instead of holding on to it.

How often do I give others the chance to lead a project/idea/event?

47.   Great leaders don't order, push or demand. They guide, lead and inspire.

How do I inspire those around me?

48. A great leader develops others
and motivates them to be the best
they can be.

Who was the last person I motivated?

49. A leader who fails under pressure has a strength that is too small for leadership.

How do I deal with stress?

50. Leaders do not quit. They get up, learn from failures and keep moving forward.

What is my attitude to failure?

51.   A leader must never feed on other people's failures, weaknesses or sorrow.

When someone I know fails, do I feel happy or sad?

Leaders don't quit.

Leading

52. Lead and teach by example.

What is the one thing that I do but would not want someone else to do because it is not good?

53. Be ready to be the fall guy to protect your team.

If someone on my team made an error of judgement, how would I react?

54. A leader honors all people.

I honor other people by

_____

_____

55. A true leader is an example to his followers.

Why would someone follow me?

Learning

56. Learn and keep learning for increased knowledge.

What new knowledge did I acquire today?

57. Read, study and learn from the histories and legacies of great leaders.

Who is your inspirational leader?

58. Train and keep training to perfect your skills.

What new skill did I learn yesterday?

59.   Keep any knowledge gained in your mental database. Use it when an opportunity arises.

What is the first leadership tip in this book?

60.   Learn from every experience
and utilize those lessons.

What did I experience today?

61. Keep a journal of lessons learnt or share them with other people to empower them.

Do I mentor young people around me?

62. Every time you use what you learn, you take a step closer to excellence.

What lessons have I learnt today that I will use in my workplace or in my relationship tomorrow?

63.   Every failure is an opportunity to learn.

What failure have I turned into an opportunity this year?

64. Every success is a step toward excellence.

How far am I from my vision or goal?

65. Never repeat the same mistake twice. Learn from it.

What mistake have I made twice? Why did I repeat the same mistake again?

66.   Reflect constantly on what and why.

Which of these leadership tips had the strongest impact on me and why?

67. Learn from the past and look forward to the future.

What mistake have I made in the past that I have never repeated? How did I avoid making the same mistake again?

68. When you are eager to learn something from everybody, your learning opportunities will be unlimited.

What did I learn from a friend today?

69. Leaders are always ready
to learn; their eyes are open for
knowledge.

*What was the last book I read apart
from this one?*

Self reflection

What will I

Stop doing

_____

_____

Start doing

_____

_____

Performance Management

70. When giving feedback, highlight strengths first.

When I'm giving someone feedback, do I start with the negative or the positive?

71. Judge actions, not people. Use statements such as, 'Your <u>action</u> affected/made/contributed etc'

Do I judge people or their actions?

72. In dealing with poor or weak performance, identify the concern, the reason, and what "I" can do to help solve the problem.

How do I help people in my team or my life to perform better?

Personal Development

73. Take the bold step of asking your team, family and peers to give you feedback on your personal values, principles and ways of working.

When was the last time someone gave me critical feedback?

74. Maximize all opportunities even if it means not getting paid but aim to gain experience.

When was the last time I volunteered my time for my community?

75. Do not aim to be the best in the world, but aim to be the best for the world (Charles Abani)

Do I put my best into everything I do?

Problem Solving

76. Focus on where you are going to and not what you are going through (Dr Edwin Louis Cole).

Is what I'm doing now going to help me to achieve my goals in life?

77. Focus on what 'I' can do in dealing or solving a problem. It makes you think creatively out of the box.

What can I do to solve the problem in my community?

78. Focus on solutions rather than the problem.

Three possible solutions for the challenge I am going through right now are;

i)_____

ii)_____

iii)_____

79. When people abuse you, do not take things personally. Let God fight your battle.

I resolve to let God fight my battles today.

80. Challenges with people could be overcome by using your influence. Just know who, when, where and what to influence.

Who are the key people to influence at my work or in my family?

Relationships

81. It's all about relationships.
Nurture value-adding relationships.

*Have I said something positive to
someone today?*

82. Surround yourself with the right people - your inner circle.

Who are in my inner circle?

83. Love others as you love yourself.

How do I demonstrate love to others?

84. Whenever you're with people, watch, listen and learn. Learn what their values, principles and passions are.

List the talents of two people close to you.

85. Know people's pressure points,
what is important and valuable to
them e.g. values, principles,
spirituality, children, family, pets
etc.

*What is most important to the person
closest to me?*

86. When you want to influence people, make their pressure points central to your point.

What makes the person closest to me get upset?

87. In business, get to know the passion of the people you relate with. Use that knowledge as an ice breaker.

What is the passion of your most important business colleague?

88. Look first for the good things in others.

Three things that I like about my best friend are

    i)_____

    ii) _____

    iii) _____

89. Seek respect through demonstrating humility and integrity.

Does my attitude reflect humility or pride?

90. Appreciate, appreciate and appreciate people some more.

Stop now and tell someone something positive.

91. See people as a "10" not a zero (John Maxwell; Million Leader's Mandate).

Do I see the good in each person I meet daily?

92. Always seek to bring out the best in people.

What can I do to bring out the best in those around me?

93. Always demonstrate loyalty and kindness.

What kind thing did I do recently?

94. Have and demonstrate compassion for people.

Am I willing to overlook the wrong done to me?

95. Use 'we' when referring to success and 'we' when referring to other's failure.

What is my attitude to other people's success or failure?

96. Do not fight other peoples'
battles. Be objective.

Do I take sides easily?

97.   If you treat others badly, you will be treated worse; if you treat them kindly you will get kinder.

Have you treated anyone badly recently? What do you need to do to make amends?

98. The heart of a leader is his or her relationship with God. Always strive to keep your conscience clear before God and man.

Do you believe in God? If no, who do you depend on?

99. Give more than you receive.

Do I put my needs first before other people's needs?

100. When a leader is always faithful, responsible and completely trustworthy, no one finds anything to criticise or condemn.

Am I always faithful?
Am I always responsible?
Am I always trustworthy?

101. Leaders add value to others.

Is my leadership adding value to others or taking value from them?

Learning is a lifelong experience.
Enrich your life's journey with the
full set of 1001 Leadership Tips
Series.

➤ Series Two 100 Leadership Tips
for Wisdom. *(Available now on
Amazon and other online
bookstores)*

www.ingramcontent.com/pod-product-compliance
Lightning Source LLC
Chambersburg PA
CBHW071513220526
45472CB00003B/1013